GW01376725

Now and Then

Eskimo snow spectacles

an elephant tooth bracelet from Africa

a comb made of moose antler from North America

These were some of the *artificial curiosities* from far-off places which tickled the curiosity of the British Museum's first visitors in the eighteenth century.

At that time, large areas of the world were still unexplored by Europeans. At the end of the eighteenth century the voyages of Captain Cook took him to the shores of Australia and to unknown Pacific islands. Everywhere he visited he studied the people and their customs and collected interesting objects. Many of these are now in the Museum of Mankind, including this image of a god which was collected by Captain Cook in Hawaii. It is made of thousands of tiny feathers tied onto netting.

During the nineteenth and twentieth centuries, the museum's collections have continued to grow. Thousands more items are still being added each year. In 1970 the over-crowded ethnographic department of the British Museum moved out into a building of its own and became the Museum of Mankind.

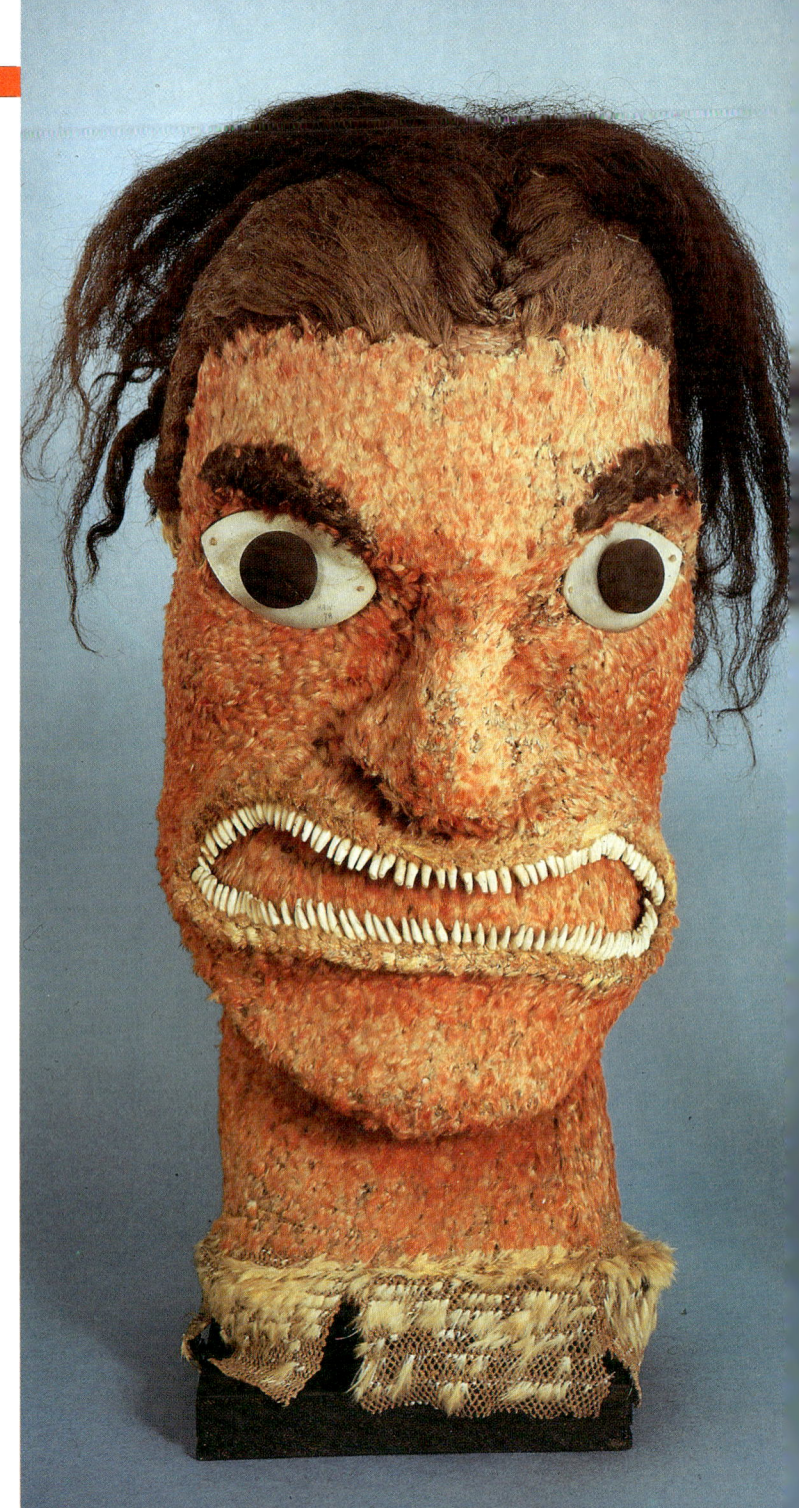

Today there are few unexplored places left. No-one remains beyond the reach of trade and machinery and the plans of powerful governments. Ways of living which had stayed much the same for centuries are now changing fast.

The Museum of Mankind is still adding to its collections in order to record traditional ways of life before they disappear. It is now studying how old customs and new ideas are fitted together. This work is carried out by anthropologists who study groups of people and how they live.

Recently, an anthropologist from the museum spent several months in Madagascar, a large island off the east coast of Africa. He worked with local people in order to collect everyday objects made in traditional ways.

The anthropologist collected medicines, made of roots and seeds, from a traditional doctor and his assistant. First he took part in a special ceremony. The doctor mixed up a concoction of all the medicines and then tasted it to show that the medicine was good.

The children were fascinated by cars and lorries although they saw very few. Their toy models are made from a material which grew in their village.

Can you guess what it is? (Answer on inside of back cover.)

The objects and information collected in Madagascar can now be used to mount an exhibition in the museum, along with rare and valuable objects lent by the University of Madagascar.

A traditional doctor and his assistant.

In the Store

The Museum of Mankind now occupies a grand and impressive building in Burlington Gardens in London. It has twelve rooms for exhibitions but there is not much space for storage. Most of the museum's objects, from poisoned arrow heads to giant canoes, are stored in a large warehouse five miles away in East London.

The museum often lends objects for exhibitions in other countries around the world. The items on the right were collected on a voyage of discovery nearly two hundred years ago. Here they are being packed into crates in layers of foam rubber, ready for a journey by lorry to the airport and then by jumbo jet to Canada.

Even for the short journey to the museum, each object must be checked and listed and carefully packed to prevent any damage on the way.

When objects first arrive at the store from abroad, they all have to be fumigated to prevent harmful insects from causing damage. The objects are packed into a large metal chamber. The air is sucked out and then a liquid gas is pumped in. The gas seeps into every nook and cranny, killing off insects, grubs and eggs. Nuts and seeds have to be pierced to stop them exploding and to prevent anything nasty from boring its way out later. When objects are on display in the museum a watch is still kept to make sure there are no moths or beetles at work eating the exhibits.

Most of the museum's objects are made of *organic* materials which come from plants or animals: wood, bark, grass, cloth, leather, bones, feather, hair and so on. All these materials contain a certain amount of water. If they dry out they become brittle and may crack or split. So to preserve the objects, the humidity (the amount of moisture in the air) has to be kept steady. Machines like the one on the right above are used in the store and in the museum. They measure the moisture in the air and blow out damp air when it is needed.

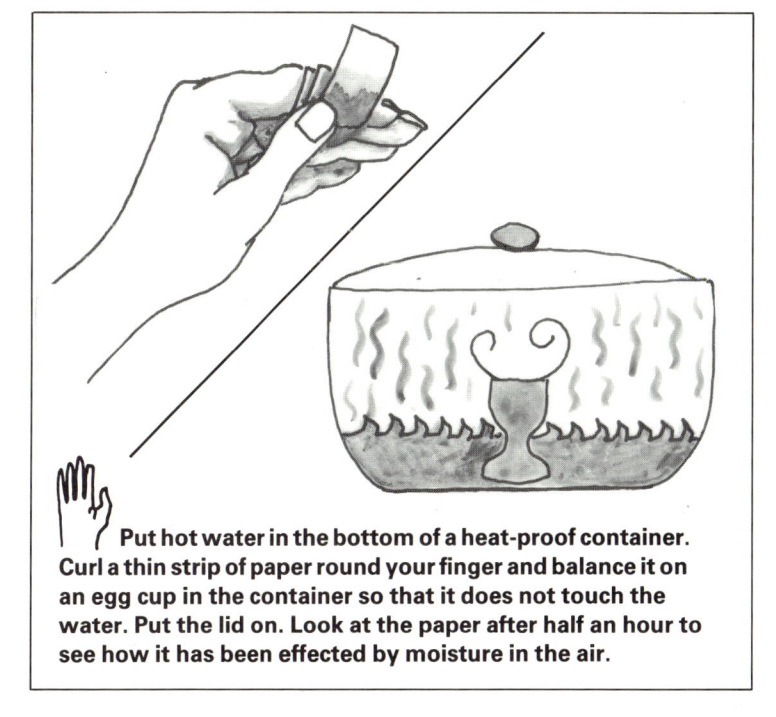

Put hot water in the bottom of a heat-proof container. Curl a thin strip of paper round your finger and balance it on an egg cup in the container so that it does not touch the water. Put the lid on. Look at the paper after half an hour to see how it has been effected by moisture in the air.

5

Running Repairs

Conservators look after the museum's objects to preserve them for the future. They clean and mend them before they are put on exhibition and work out ways of displaying them safely.

The human head below was shrunk and preserved in the Amazon jungle at the turn of this century. It was kept by a warrior who thought that the head, and especially the hair, would give him power over his enemies. Now museum conservators continue to preserve it so that you can see what it was like. Before it was put on exhibition recently the face and the hair were cleaned with methylated spirits and detergent. The head had to be kept mounted on a stand with the jawbone supported.

The conservator above is working on a feather *headdress*. She picks up the feathers with tweezers and very carefully smooths them with a fine paintbrush.

When objects like this are put on display they have to be kept away from the light as bright colours fade easily. That is why the exhibition rooms in the museum are kept fairly dark and have no windows.

To repair objects properly, conservators need to find out all they can about how they were made in the first place.

This magnificent mourner's dress was brought back from Tahiti two hundred years ago by Captain Cook. A few years ago conservators took it all apart to investigate how it was made and to carry out repairs. Each part of the dress needed different treatment.

To everyone's surprise, when the headdress was taken off this little wooden man was found inside, propping it up. It was the kind of figure used by sorcerers to help them with their magic.

Each feather was washed with water and gently smoothed back into shape.

The cord around the neck is made of barkcloth string. It was taken off and treated to preserve the fibres.

This pendant is made of 2,500 pieces of shiny pearl shell. New pieces were cut to fill the gaps. Other pieces needed sticking with glue.

The feather ornaments had been nibbled by moths and had to be repaired very carefully.

The main part of the dress is made of bark cloth. Special fluids were used to clean it and to mat the fibres together.

? **Can you guess what these are made of? (Answer on inside of back cover)**

Organising an Exhibition

A lot of work goes on behind the scenes before an exhibition can be opened to the public. The planning and building can take several years.

Recently, it was decided to mount an exhibition to show what life is like in an Indian village. First of all, an anthropologist from the museum travelled to India and discussed the project with Indian experts. Together they visited villages in Gujarat taking photographs, collecting everyday objects and talking to local people. Indians living in Britain gave advice.

Designers drew up plans for the building of an Indian village street inside the museum.

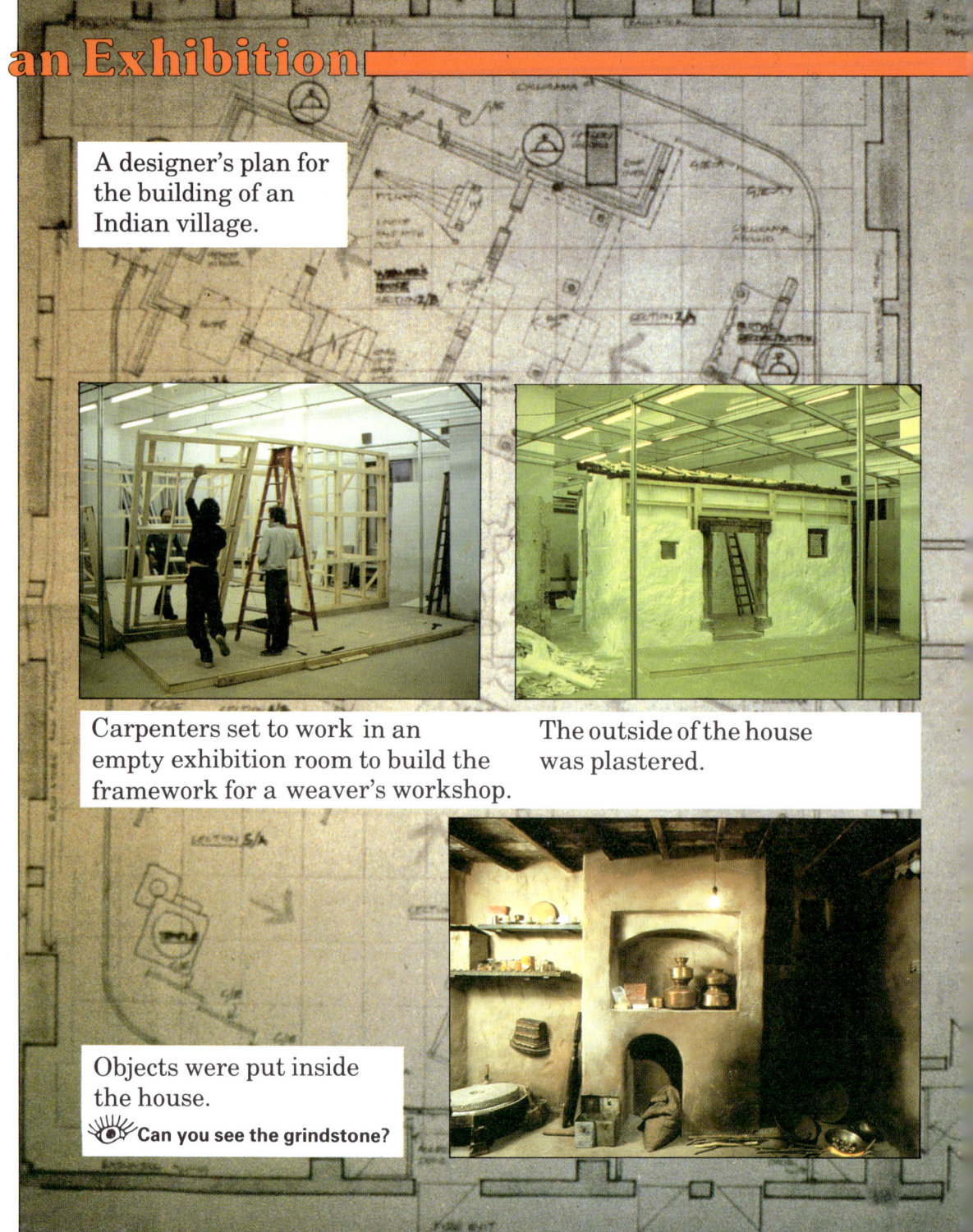

A designer's plan for the building of an Indian village.

Carpenters set to work in an empty exhibition room to build the framework for a weaver's workshop.

The outside of the house was plastered.

Objects were put inside the house.
Can you see the grindstone?

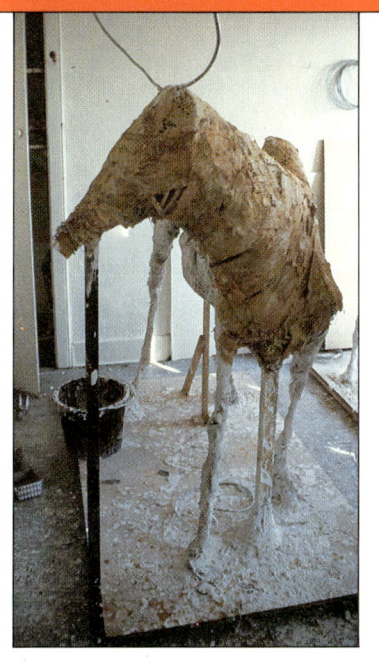

People in Gujarat still use carts pulled by bullocks. A cart was brought back from India, but there were no bullocks to pull it so models had to be made.

The bullocks were made of chicken wire and fibre-glass in a sculptor's studio.

The only way to get the finished bullocks out of the building was through the window.

They were carried up the steps into the Museum of Mankind to join the exhibition.

Once the village street was complete and the bullock cart was in place, the exhibition opened to the public and thousands of visitors came to see it.

Map of the World

Use this map and key to discover where the objects in this book come from.

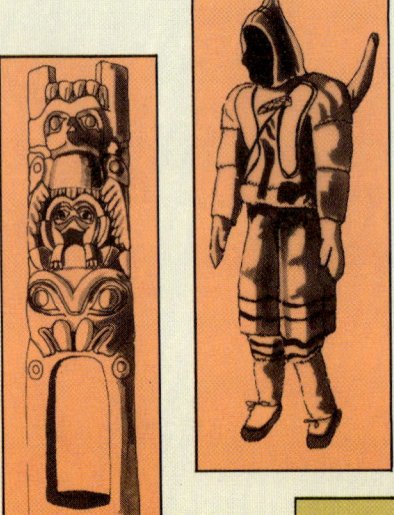

ALASKA
CANADA
GREENLAND
ARCTIC
NORTH AMERICA
GREAT BRITAIN
London
Central Plains
ATLANTIC OCEAN
HAWAII
MEXICO
GHANA
NIG
PACIFIC OCEAN
Amazon River
SOUTH AMERICA
COOK ISLANDS
TAHITI

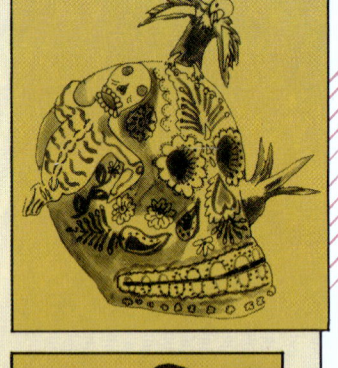

KEY
NORTH AMERICA
SOUTH AMERICA
AFRICA
ASIA
OCEANIA

MIDDLE EAST
Gujarat
INDIA
MALAYSIA
KIRIBATI ISLANDS
JAVA
NEW GUINEA
INDIAN OCEAN
MADAGASCAR
PACIFIC OCEAN
AUSTRALIA

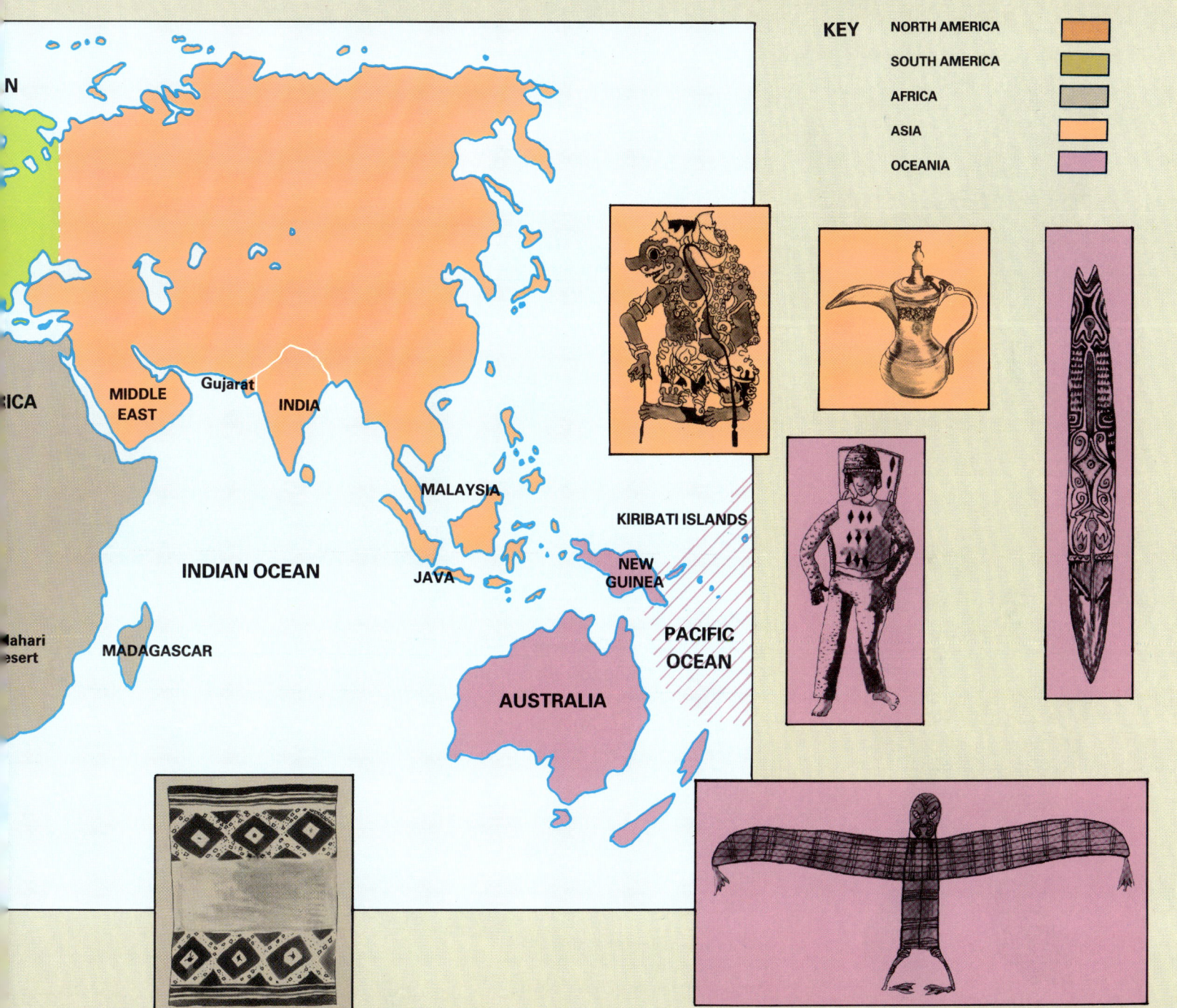

11

Surviving in a Cold Climate

Eskimos (or Inuit as most of them call themselves) live along the Arctic coastlines of Greenland and North America. They know more than anyone else in the world about how to survive in a cold climate. For thousands of years they have hunted and travelled and kept themselves warm and well-fed through long, dark, frozen winters.

The men who wore these clothes were able to keep warm in temperatures far colder than the inside of a freezer. The man's outfit is made from caribou fur and the trousers are made of polar-bear skin. The fur traps air which is warmed by the body and stops cold air from penetrating.

For much of the year the ground and even the sea is frozen solid and covered with snow. For travelling over the ice and snow the Eskimos used sledges pulled by dogs.

Today they use snow mobiles. These travel on caterpillar tracks which move across the snow more easily than wheels.

? **Can you guess what this sledge is made of?**
(Answer on inside of back cover.)

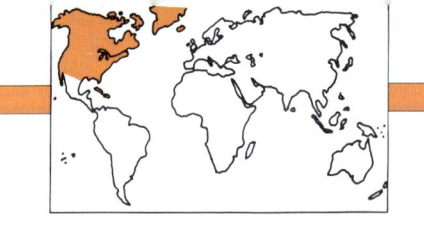

Through the Stomach of a Raven

This massive carved doorway was built into the front of a large Indian house on the west coast of Canada. It used to be brightly coloured but the paint has now worn off.

Everyone went in and out through the stomach of the raven at the bottom. This carving was the badge of the most senior chief living in the house and represented his spirit ancestors. The other carvings had special meanings too, telling stories of the ancient past and showing the chief's present importance.

Can you identify the creature at the top? (Answer on inside of back cover.)

Totem poles could be built into the houses, like this doorway, or they could stand outside as monuments to famous chiefs. Sometimes they were used as grave markers with the coffin sitting on top of the pole.

Totem poles were only ever made along the Northwest coast of North America. The Indians did not need to travel far in search of fish and so were able to build permanent houses. They built huge canoes for fishing and developed great skill in carving.

There are still many Indian carvers on the Northwest coast. Recently a giant tree trunk was shipped to Britain from Alaska and Indians spent five weeks carving a totem pole in the Museum of Mankind.

Warrior Headdress

This feather headdress belonged to Yellow Calf, the last chief of the Arapaho tribe, who died in 1938. It is decorated with fur and the feathers are tipped with horsehair.

The Indians living on the great central plains of America lived by hunting. They used horses, which were introduced by the Spanish three hundred years ago, to chase bison.

War was an important part of life, and successful warriors won power and respect within the tribe. Many daring deeds involved the stealing of horses, which were so important for hunting.

Warriors were able to *keep the score* of their successes by feathers in their headdresses and decorations on their clothing. War honours helped to give men power and they took part in many ceremonies and sacred rituals in order to increase this power.

Counting the Years

The Dakota Indians spoke a language which they did not write down. In order to count the years and to record special events in their history they kept a Winter Count. This one is made of cloth and the pictographs are drawn in black ink. Each winter a new pictograph was added showing an event by which the past year would be remembered.

This Winter Count was kept from 1758-1901.

Can you find the pictograph for the year when
1. There were star showers from a meteor?
2. There was a smallpox epidemic?
3. Snow shoes were needed for hunting?
4. Sniffer shot a white buffalo?

(Answers on inside of back cover.)

Make your own count on a piece of plain cloth or paper. Use black ink, felt tip pen or a fine paintbrush to draw pictographs for each year of your life. Start in the top right-hand corner and move round in an anti-clockwise spiral like this. You could try recording your family's history, starting in the year a parent or grandparent was born.

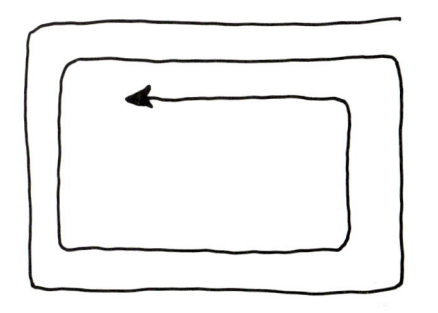

Maya Hieroglyphs

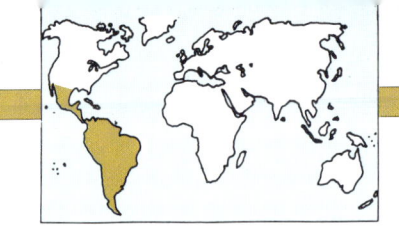

While the Roman Empire was spreading across Europe, the Maya Indians were developing their civilisation in Middle America. Among the trees and jungle undergrowth they built splendid temples and palaces. They carved the stone surfaces of their monuments with pictures and writing which told the story of their past.

A hundred years ago, Alfred Maudslay became fascinated by the remains of Maya civilisation. He set out to make a record of the monuments which survived, ruined and overgrown in the jungle, so that scholars could make a proper study of Maya art and writing.

Many of the enormous stones could not be moved, so he collected the inscriptions on them by covering their surfaces with wet plaster or paper. When these moulds were dry they were taken off and brought back to England. They were used to make replicas of the original stones. A replica now stands by the stairs in the Museum of Mankind.

Maya languages are still spoken today, but no-one has yet fully worked out the meanings of the old hieroglyphs. We know that the bars and dots are numbers showing calendar dates which the Maya recorded very accurately.

What numbers can you spot in these hieroglyphs?

Clue: ●●●● / ▬ = 9

(Answers on inside of back cover.)

The Day of the Dead

Each year on 2 November, people in Mexico celebrate the Day of the Dead. They set up altars in their homes and put out the favourite foods of friends and relations who have died recently. Models of skulls are used to decorate the altars. The magnificent skull on the right was moulded out of *papier mâché*.

Each year sugar skulls like this are made from a paste of sugar and water. They can be placed on altars as food for the dead or they may be given away as presents, rather like our Easter eggs. Children look forward to being given a sugar skull from the altar to eat.

👁 **Can you see the child's name on the skull below?**

In some villages, trails of yellow petals are laid leading from each house towards the church. Yellow is the ancient colour of death and the petals lead the spirits back to the cemetery after their visit to the house.

The Day of the Dead is the Christian festival of All Souls Day (the day after Hallowe'en). In Mexico the festival also has links with older Indian traditions, as with the Aztec religious ceremonies where skulls and masks, such as the turquoise mosaic on the cover, were used.

Hidden People

The Amazon River is the largest river in the world. It flows through a huge area of forest, ten times the size of Britain. For many thousands of years, groups of Indians have lived hidden away in the dense forest, richly supplied with fish, meat and fruit from their surroundings.

Now, with the building of roads and airstrips and the cutting down of large areas of forest, the Indians are no longer sealed off from the outside world. As they come into contact with new ways of doing things, the old ways are in danger of being lost.

The men are skilled hunters. They shoot animals such as deer and fish with bows and arrows which are sometimes tipped with poison. Shotguns are widely used nowadays, but birds and monkeys are still often killed with darts puffed silently from long blowguns.

The Indians have a deep knowledge of plants and their uses. They make a deadly poison called *curare* from a vine plant. When a poison-tipped arrow or dart pierces the skin of an animal it dies almost immediately. The poison paralyses it so that it cannot breathe. The meat can still be eaten because the poison does not work if taken by mouth.

Scientists were fascinated when they learned about this Indian poison. They worked out how to use it for making drugs to relax people's muscles during operations.

👁 This man is painting the front of a large house in which a group of Indians live together. The paint is in a gourd. Can you see what he is using as a paintbrush?

There is little need for clothes in the heat and damp of the forest, but men, women and children decorate themselves with bracelets, anklets and necklaces of beads and teeth. Sometimes they paint their bodies, using red and black colours made from plants. Black is to do with death and coldness. Red stands for heat and life.

Boys and girls go through ceremonies to mark the end of childhood and the beginning of adult life. Their bodies are specially painted for this important occasion.

✋ Spread out a large piece of paper. Lie down on it and ask a friend to draw round you. Cut out your shape. Paint patterns on the face and body using red and black paint.
The picture on this page will help you to plan your designs.

As contact grows with the outside world, more and more Indians are wearing European-style clothes such as shirts and trousers or skirts.

Glistening Gold

In 1817 a group of Britons visited the kingdom of Asante in West Africa. As they entered the capital city they saw an amazing sight.

'The sun was reflected...from the gold ornaments which glittered in every direction. The chiefs wore massy gold intricately wrought...a band of gold encircled the knee... small circles of gold were strung round their ankles... rocks of lump gold hung from their wrists... Gold...dazzled the eye in every direction.'

For hundreds of years, gold was found in large quantities on Africa's *Gold Coast*, which is now Ghana. Asante goldsmiths made magnificent ornaments to adorn the king and his high officials.

This is the method they used:
1. Model the shape in beeswax
2. Coat the model with clay and drill a hole to the wax
3. Heat the mould so that the wax melts and runs out
4. Run liquid gold into the empty mould
5. Cool it and then smash off the clay
6. Clean and polish the solid gold ornament

The King of Asante's gold ornaments are extremely valuable. When they were displayed in the museum they had to be locked in showcases.

Technicians had the job of making replica jewellery which would look as realistic as possible.

They made this amulet.

👁 Can you guess what they used? (Answer on inside of back cover.)

This model was set up in the museum to show how the jewellery was worn.

Can you see the amulet?

Living Simply

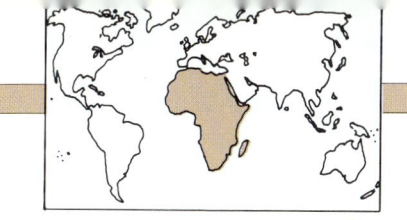

About 10,000 years ago, man first began to learn how to grow crops and to keep animals. Until then, all our ancestors lived by hunting wild animals and gathering food from wild plants.

This ancient way of life is still carried on by the San, who used to be called Bushmen. They now survive only in remote parts of the Kalahari desert in Southern Africa. Even there the twentieth century is fast catching up with them.

The San have few possessions. They live in the open, building simple shelters of brushwood and grass. When food is needed the men go hunting. The women gather nuts, berries and fruits and dig up tasty roots from the ground. If food runs short they move on.

Water is precious and has to be saved. This decorated ostrich egg makes a tough water container. It was filled and buried in the ground and dug up again later when water was needed. The covered gourd was used for carrying water on journeys. In Summer when the water-holes dry up, thirst can be quenched by sucking water melons.

The San live simply but their customs and beliefs are rich and complicated. In the evening they gather around their camp fires to talk and tell stories. In this way they pass on to their children the wisdom they have gathered over the centuries.

Zulu Warriors

About a thousand years ago the Zulu settled down in a hilly grassland area of southern Africa, where they could herd cattle and grow crops. At that time there were only a few thousand Zulu. Today there are four million.

The Zulu became fierce warriors. They attacked and won over other clans in this part of Africa and in this way they grew bigger. They resisted the white settlers who arrived in the nineteenth century. In 1879, though they had no guns they wiped out an invading British army, and stories of Zulu bravery and ferocity spread around the world.

This Zulu shield helped to protect the man who carried it from almost head to toe.

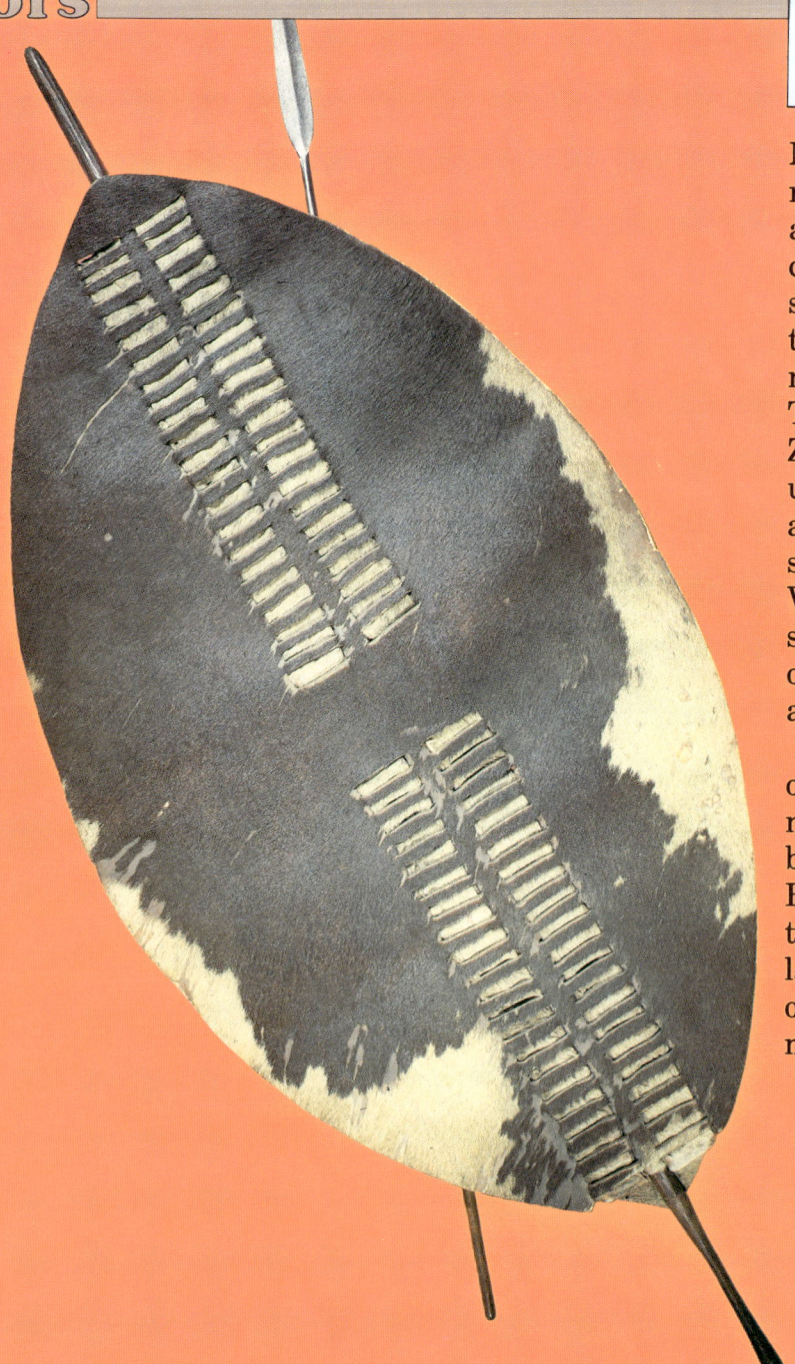

Men in different regiments of the Zulu army carried different coloured shields. These shields were cut from tough ox hide and could not be pierced by spears. This meant that the Zulu warrior could get up close to the enemy and attack him with a short stabbing spear. Warriors showed their success by the number of ox-tails they wore tied around their bodies.

Zululand is now part of South Africa and many Zulu travel to the big towns to find work. But the Zulu remember that they belong to a large family with its own long traditions and modern customs.

Patterns on Cloth

In Nigeria and many other parts of Africa, cotton cloth for clothing is *resist-dyed* to produce striking patterns. The patterns shown here were made by tying or stitching the plain cloth with raffia before it was dyed. Raffia is made from the fibres of palm leaves. It resists the dye and stops it from penetrating the cloth.

The most widely used dye is indigo, a blue dye prepared from the leaves of the indigo plant. Leaf balls are mixed with water in dye pots sunk into the ground. The dye produces colours ranging from light blue to nearly black.

Try your hand at tie-and-die. Use plain white cotton cloth (eg a handkerchief, a T-shirt or a piece of sheeting).

You can make lines by pleating the cloth and tying the folds with string.

Wrap the string round the cloth tightly and neatly so that the dye cannot seep through. You can make wide lines or narrow lines.

You can make circles by putting stones into the cloth and tying round them.

Dye your cloth in a cold water dye such as Dylon following the instructions on the tin.

23

A House of Hair

The Bedouin live in desert areas of the Middle East. Many have now settled in villages and work in the towns. Some still lead a nomadic way of life, moving from place to place in search of food and water for their animals. Their wealth consists of herds of sheep and goats and camels. These animals provide them with milk and meat to eat, skins for leather, dung for fuel, and wool and hair for cloth.

The Bedouin name for tent is *house of hair*. Tents are made of strips of black cloth which are woven from goat hair and sheep wool. The women spin the yarn and do the weaving. They weave long strips of cloth on looms stretched out on the ground like this. Strips are sewn together to make the tent roof. The walls are made separately and are pinned onto the roof.

A woven curtain is hung up inside the tent to divide it into two parts. On one side the men do their business and entertain visitors. The other side is for sleeping and for the women and children to live in during the day.

Visitors are always made welcome and treated with great courtesy. The Bedouin have few possessions, but magnificent coffee sets such as this show the importance attached to entertaining guests.

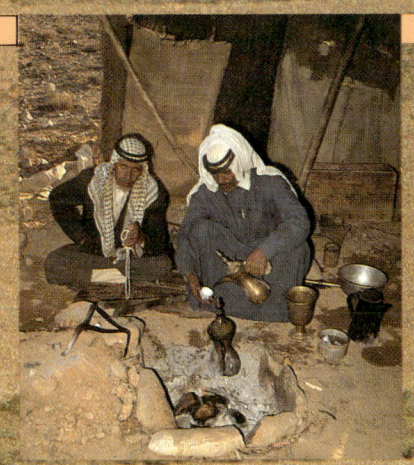

Coffee is served with great ceremony as a sign of the host's duty to give friendship and protection to anyone who enters his home.

Coffee beans are roasted on the fire, crushed with a pestle and mortar, and thrown into boiling water in the largest coffee pot. From there the coffee is strained into smaller and smaller pots before being poured into tiny cups. Guest's cups are filled three times and then it is polite to refuse any more.

Guests sit around the hearth in the men's section, on cushions and rugs. Women are supposed to keep out of sight, but they often listen in from behind the curtain and may even peer over or shout comments of their own.

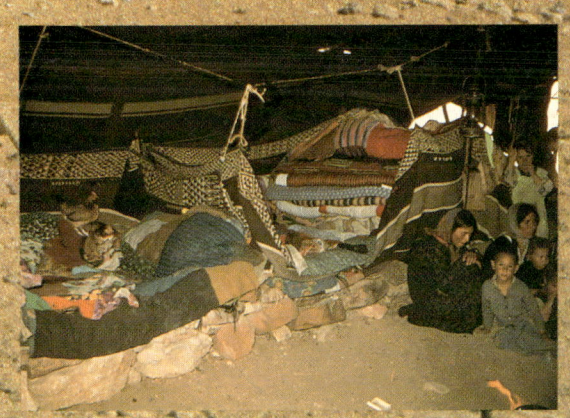

Can you see the bedding piled up against the dividing curtain on the women's side?

Shadow Puppets

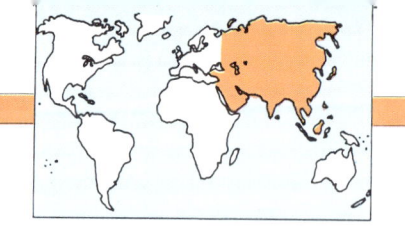

Shadow plays are still performed in South East Asia. The puppets are held up against a white sheet with a light behind them. They make shadows on the screen which can be seen from the other side. The audience soon gets caught up in the story, watching the dancing shadows and listening to the puppet-master's voices. Excitement mounts as the Rama makes his entry. A great struggle follows between forces of good and evil. This finally brings about the rescue of Rama's love Sita.

The stories are complicated, but they are well known by the audience. Everyone recognises the gods and giants, kings and princes, beasts and ogres as they appear, and understands the good and bad qualities they represent.

This shadow puppet is Rama, the hero of the shadow play. It is one of a large group collected by Sir Stamford Raffles when he was Governor of Java in the early nineteenth century. It is marvellously detailed and must have been made by very skilful craftsmen, perhaps for use at a royal court.

Shadow puppets are made from animal hide. The skin is scraped, stretched and dried to make smooth thin sheets of parchment. The craftsman then cuts out the puppet's outline. He uses sharp-edged chisels to make the patterns of holes which let the light through.

The puppets are painted with special colours for each character, decorated with gold leaf and varnished. Pieces of horn are shaped and bent to support the puppet and to form a long handle for the puppet-master to hold. The arms are jointed and can be moved with the help of thin sticks attached to the hands. The puppet-master certainly has his hands full, but he is amazingly skilful in bringing the puppets to life.

Make your own shadow puppets.
Draw people or animals on thin card and cut them out. Show details by pushing a nail through the card to make holes or by cutting out strips with scissors. Clip a clothes peg to the bottom of each puppet to make a handle.

Fix a screen of white paper or sheeting across a doorway. Turn out the lights, draw the curtains and shine a reading lamp or a torch onto the screen. Hold your puppets up against the screen with the light behind them. Make up their voices and tell a story as you move them about.

Coconut Armour

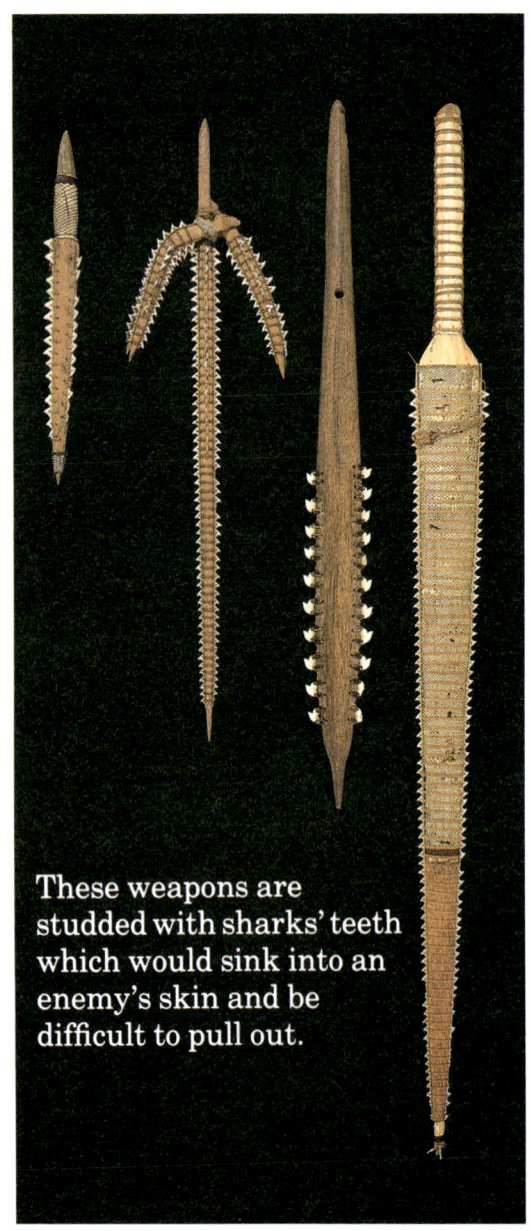

These weapons are studded with sharks' teeth which would sink into an enemy's skin and be difficult to pull out.

The people of the Pacific Islands did not learn how to use metals until they came into contact with Europeans. They made everything they needed, including tools, weapons and armour, from stone, plant and animal materials which were readily available.

On Kiribati, a group of islands in the middle of the Pacific Ocean, war against neighbouring islanders was a popular occupation. It was important to be well prepared.

The suit of armour protected its wearer from shark tooth weapons like these on the left. It is made of brown fibres which were collected from coconut shells and plaited together by hand.

Magical Masks

In New Guinea, as in many other parts of the world, boys go through special rituals to mark the end of childhood and the beginning of manhood. *Initiated* men share in the secrets of the spirit world, and learn the uses of sacred objects such as these.

Men dress up in masks like this one on the right to perform ceremonial dances. In their disguise they appear to be powerful spirits, towering over ordinary people. Spirit voices can be heard too. The sound is really made by instruments like this bull-roarer on the left. It moans loudly when it is swung round in the air on a piece of string.

The mask has a long grass skirt to hide the person inside. The top part is made of barkcloth. This material is widely used on Pacific Islands where there is no cotton or wool. The inner bark of trees is stripped off and soaked and pounded until the fibres mesh together like felt. Barkcloth can be painted, so it is useful for decoration as well as for making clothes.

Make your own mask
Roll a sheet of thin card to make a cone which will fit over your head and rest on your shoulders. Stick down the seam and trim the bottom edge. Make small eye-holes and paint patterns around them. Cut long strips of brown paper or newspaper for the skirt. Stick down the ends inside the rim of the cone so that the strips hang down and hide your body.

Money with a Difference

Almost anything can be used as money so long as people agree on its value and are happy to accept it in exchange for the goods they are selling. On the Pacific Islands, money took many different forms.

In one area these large round stones were used. They could be as little as thirty centimetres or as large as four metres across. They were so heavy that they had to be carried around on poles, which is why they have holes in the middle. A small stone might buy an axe but a rather larger stone would be needed to pay for a pig. Women used shells as small change.

On some islands pigs' tails were highly prized. The pig-money on the left below is made of strings of shells with pigs' tails on the ends.

This small object was used in the making of feather money.

? Can you guess what it is?
(Answer on inside of back cover.)

Feather money was made in a coil about ten metres long. Scales of feathers were overlapped along a ribbon of string. Each scale was made from doves' feathers surrounded by tiny red feathers from honey-birds. Four or five hundred birds were plucked to make a coil. It would only have been used to get something important such as a wife or a new canoe.

Bird-Man

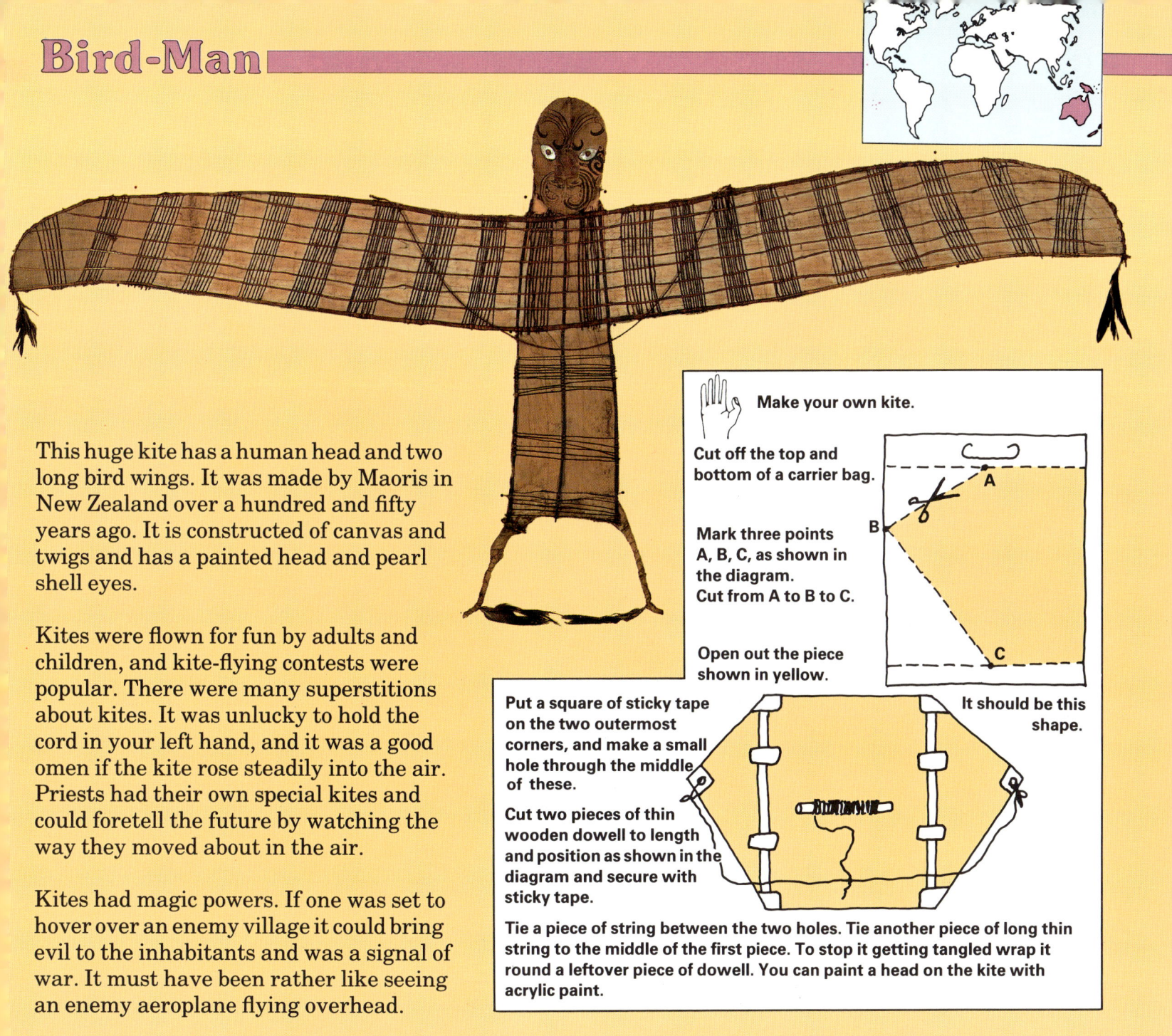

This huge kite has a human head and two long bird wings. It was made by Maoris in New Zealand over a hundred and fifty years ago. It is constructed of canvas and twigs and has a painted head and pearl shell eyes.

Kites were flown for fun by adults and children, and kite-flying contests were popular. There were many superstitions about kites. It was unlucky to hold the cord in your left hand, and it was a good omen if the kite rose steadily into the air. Priests had their own special kites and could foretell the future by watching the way they moved about in the air.

Kites had magic powers. If one was set to hover over an enemy village it could bring evil to the inhabitants and was a signal of war. It must have been rather like seeing an enemy aeroplane flying overhead.

Make your own kite.

Cut off the top and bottom of a carrier bag.

Mark three points A, B, C, as shown in the diagram.
Cut from A to B to C.

Open out the piece shown in yellow.

It should be this shape.

Put a square of sticky tape on the two outermost corners, and make a small hole through the middle of these.

Cut two pieces of thin wooden dowell to length and position as shown in the diagram and secure with sticky tape.

Tie a piece of string between the two holes. Tie another piece of long thin string to the middle of the first piece. To stop it getting tangled wrap it round a leftover piece of dowell. You can paint a head on the kite with acrylic paint.

31

Museum of Mankind Quiz

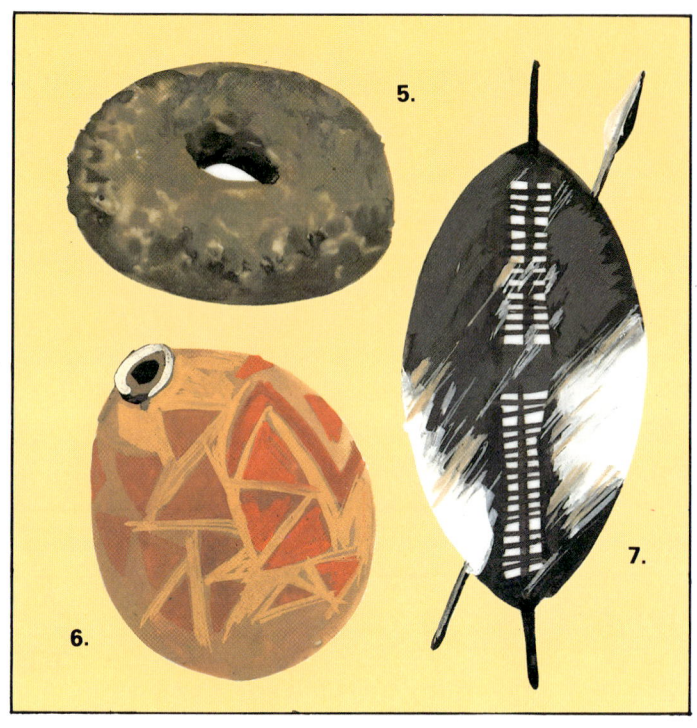

Each of these faces comes from an object shown in the guide. Can you recognise them all?

What was each of these objects used for?

8. Most of the objects in the museum are made of natural materials. This square contains the names of four animal and four plant materials mentioned in the guide. Find each one by moving up, down, across or diagonally from one letter to the next.

(Answers on inside of back cover.)

S	L	L	E	H
N	K	D	B	S
I	L	O	S	A
N	W	O	M	R
E	O	B	G	K